SO-DUI-292

DELETE THIS BOOK
from Jerabek School Library

Artistic Adventures
PEN PALS

Kelly Burkholder

JERABEK SCHOOL
10050 Avenida Magnifica
San Diego, CA 92131
578-5330

The Rourke Press, Inc.
Vero Beach, Florida 32964

© 2001 The Rourke Press, Inc.
All rights reserved. No part of this book may be reproduced or utilized
in any form or by any means, electronic or mechanical including photocopying, recording, or by any
information storage and retrieval system without permission in writing from the publisher.

PHOTO CREDITS
© East Coast Studios: cover, pages 6, 12, 13, 17, 19, 21; © Eyewire: page 4; © Glenn Benson: page 9;
© PhotoDisc: pages 10, 14, 22

PRODUCED & DESIGNED by East Coast Studios
eastcoaststudios.com

EDITORIAL SERVICES
Pamela Schroeder

Library of Congress Cataloging-in-Publication Data

Burkholder, Kelly, 1970-
    Pen pals / Kelly Burkholder.
        p. cm. — (Artistic adventures)
    Includes index.
    ISBN 1-57103-353-X
    1. Pen pals—Juvenile literature. [1. Pen pals.] I. Title.

LB3614 .B87 2000
372.62'3—dc21

                                                                    00–028434

Printed in the USA

Contents

Why Have a Pen Pal?

Pen pals are a great way to make lifelong friends. They teach you about different ways of life. You might even be able to visit your pen pal in another country or city. Pen pals help you practice writing and **communication** (ka MYOO ne KAY shun). Pen pals are a great **hobby** (HOB ee). You can have fun writing letters to your friends. It is also nice to get a letter with warm wishes and friendly words.

Friendships that begin at a young age can last a lifetime.

What to Write

When you write to a pen pal for the first time, make sure you tell them who you are and why you are writing. Tell your pen pal your **nickname** (NIK naym) or first name. Also tell them how old you are, if you are a boy or a girl, and where you live. Let your pen pal know what you like to do for fun. Tell your pen pal **details** (DEE taylz). Write "I like to read." Then add, "My favorite kind of books are scary ones." Now your pen pal can see if you have the same **interests** (IN ter ests).

It is exciting to receive mail from a friend.

Ask your pen pal to write back. You could write, "I can't wait to hear all about your camping trip." End your letters with something friendly like, "Your new friend, Matthew" or "Cheers, Matthew."

When your pen pal writes back you might say, "What do I write now?" Here are a few things to put in your letters: hobbies, sports, crafts, games, books, your school, movie stars, music, athletes, things you collect, vacations, holiday plans, or the country and state you live in. Try to ask at least one question every time you write your pen pal. Then your pen pal will write back.

Favorite hobbies or sports are good topics to write about to a pen pal.

Safety First

Be safe when you pick a pen pal. You can't always tell if your pen pal is really a good person. Tell your parents everything. Don't give out your full name unless your parents know. Never meet your new friend in real life unless you ask your parents. Always tell your parents if your pen pal makes you feel bad or strange. Many pen pals are good people, but it is important to be safe.

Tell your parents who you are writing to so they can make sure you are safe.

Making a Friend

A great way to turn your pen pal into a friend is to talk about your differences. You can teach each other about many things. Send **recipe** (RES ih pee) cards, baseball cards, bookmarks, poems, or stories. You can make things to send to your pen pal.

Share something you like with your pen pal.

Talking on the phone helps strengthen friendships.

You might even call your pen pal. First, get your parents' **permission** (per MISH un). It is a good idea to have your parents call first. They can talk to your pen pal's parents and make sure everything is okay. If your pen pal lives close by, ask your parents to set up a time to meet. Meet at a fun place, like a park or a favorite place to eat.

JERABEK SCHOOL
10050 Avenida Magnific
San Diego, CA 92131
578-5330

pen pals

13

Too Busy to Write

Sometimes you get very busy. You have school, vacations, and sports. Your pen pal may be busy with these things, too. You may not always have time to write. Hang in there. When things slow down, you can write again.

You and your pen pal might not write because you are bored. Maybe nothing new is going on. You don't have anything new to write about. Just wait a few more days to write.

School is very important and requires a lot of time.

If you are worried about how your pen pal is doing, write and ask politely how they are. You might write, "Hi, Dawn. It has been a long time since I heard from you. I hope that you are okay and nothing bad has happened. Please write to me when you have the time. Take care, Beth."

Writing to your pen pal shows that you care about the friendship.

Sending Presents

Presents are a nice idea to send to your pen pal at holidays and special times. Make sure your parents know what you are doing. Presents do not have to be big or cost a lot. The best gifts are gifts you make. Some gifts that will make your pen pal happy are pictures, friendship books, bookmarks, postcards, **stationery** (STAY shu NAYR ee), music, or stickers.

Always remember that your friendship is the most important thing. You don't have to send your pen pal presents. Mostly send letters and build your friendship with writing.

It is nice to remember special holidays and birthdays.

E-Mail

Another way to stay in touch with your pen pal is through electronic mail. Electronic mail is also called e-mail. You use a computer to send messages. It is nice to use e-mail. You do not have to spend money on stamps. You also can send and receive letters very quickly. It only takes a few minutes for an e-mail message to be received. You don't have to wait for the mail to come to find a friendly letter. However, you and your pen pal do need computers. Check with your parents to see if you are able to use e-mail.

E-mail is a great way to stay in touch with pen pals.

Glossary

communication (ka MYOO ne KAY shun) — sharing ideas through writing, speaking, and many other ways

details (DEE taylz) — facts that tell you more about someone or something

hobby (HOB ee) — something you do for fun

interests (IN ter ests) — something you like to learn about or do

nickname (NIK naym) — a special name that is given to you by your friends or family

permission (per MISH un) — being allowed to do something you want to do

recipe (RES ih pee) — instructions on how to make a meal

stationery (STAY shu NAYR ee) — paper and pens used to write letters

Share your ideas about school, family, and friends with your pen pal.

Index

Further Reading

Find out more about pen pals with these helpful information sites:

www.epals.com
www.kidlink.org
www.kidscom.com